Original title:
The Meaning of Life (Spoiler: It's Complicated)

Copyright © 2025 Creative Arts Management OÜ
All rights reserved.

Author: Jameson Hartfield
ISBN HARDBACK: 978-1-80566-282-2
ISBN PAPERBACK: 978-1-80566-577-9

Labors of the Heart

We search for love like children seek,
In candy stores with sweets to peak.
Yet finding joy in tangled strings,
Can lead to laughter and complex things.

We fill our lives with silly quests,
Like chasing dreams in goofy vests.
Each heart a puzzle, pieces lost,
But often worth the silly cost.

Portraits of Paradox

Life's a canvas, colors clash,
We paint our whims and dreams that flash.
With strokes of joy and dabs of gloom,
Our art of living fills the room.

In laughter's echo, wisdom hides,
With every giggle, truth abides.
A riddle wrapped in a teasing smile,
Unfolds the journey, takes a while.

Navigating the Abyss

We sail through waters dark and deep,
With rubber duckies, dreams to keep.
The seas of doubt can rock the boat,
Yet we still laugh and keep afloat.

With maps of stars that shift and quake,
We search for paths that seldom break.
A joke amid the stormy rain,
Keeps spirits high through bliss and pain.

Moments Laced with Meaning

In whispers shared on park bench seats,
We chase the truth 'midst funny feats.
A cozy chat, some giggles light,
Transforming chaos into light.

With cookies baked and stories spun,
In every bite, the joy's begun.
Life's tasty morsels, sweet and strange,
Help us embrace the wild exchange.

Uncharted Waters of Feeling

In oceans deep where laughter flows,
We sail on boats of mismatched shoes.
Jellyfish jokes that no one knows,
And shark attacks of silly news.

The tides shift with absurd delight,
Mermaid dreams and pirate schemes.
A cannonball of pure moonlight,
Splashing into goofy streams.

Navigating through giggles and glee,
With compasses spun a tad off track.
In the whirlpool of silly spree,
We find our way, but never look back.

Colors of a Broken Spectrum

In a world where socks never pair,
The rainbow's bent and slightly wrong.
Where orange laughs at anxious glare,
And violet hums a silly song.

Crayons melt in the summer sun,
Pastel dreams of globby goo.
Canvas fights with paint for fun,
A masterpiece of mixed-up hue.

Funny shades of life display,
Like dancing jelly on a plate.
Each color whispers, 'Come and play!'
Just be warned of fate's childlike state.

Sifting Through Sandcastles

Building towers of sandy dreams,
With moats filled with jellybeans.
The tide comes in, or so it seems,
Leaving only half-naked queens.

Buckets tipped and laughter spills,
As seagulls steal what little remains.
Sand between our toes fulfills,
The tickle of our playful pains.

In every grain, a story lies,
Of smiling suns and crabs that dance.
We sift our hopes, and then we cry,
For lost treasures in a child's glance.

The Melodies We Forget to Sing

In a world where notes just disappear,
We whistle tunes that miss their mark.
With every laugh, we draw near,
Yet lose the chorus in the dark.

A symphony of clumsy sounds,
Where every beat is out of time.
We hop on rhythms that confound,
Creating chaos in our rhyme.

So here's to songs we'll never play,
Like karaoke in the rain.
Let's harmonize our quirky way,
And dance through laughter and through pain.

Whispered Truths in Silence

In shadows we giggle, in daylight we ponder,
Life's riddle is hefty, it makes our hearts wander.
We search for the answers in cereal boxes,
Finding deep truths in our favorite sockses.

Wisdom hides under the couch with lost snacks,
It teases and dances, then swiftly it cracks.
We question our purpose while snacking on chips,
And wonder if cats know the secret of trips.

Celestial Conversations

Stars wink and they twinkle with secrets to share,
They giggle at mortals who stop and stare.
With comets as messengers, bright moonlight's a guide,
They plot out our journeys, both silly and wide.

Aliens phone home while sipping on tea,
They chuckle at humans, 'What could that be?'
Life's puzzle is quirky, a cosmic arcade,
With piñatas of wisdom where laughter's displayed.

Through the Kaleidoscope

Turn, twist, and peek through our colorful lens,
Life's not just a puzzle; it's a dance with friends.
We hop on the merry-go-round of delight,
But sometimes it stops, and we lose track of night.

Shapes slide and collide, a cacophony bright,
With patterns of sandwich that dance in delight.
Confetti of moments, we throw in the air,
In search of great meaning found everywhere.

Life's Intricate Weave

Threads intertwine, both tangled and neat,
In stitches of laughter, we find our own beat.
Life's fabric is funny, with patches of glee,
A quilt of confusion, knit comfort for free.

Sewing our hopes with a needle of dreams,
We patch up our lives with whatever it seems.
In laughter and chaos, we color our thread,
With patterns of joy that dance in our head.

The Balance of Chaos

In a world of topsy-turvy, we spin around,
Juggling dreams and laundry on the ground.
We laugh at fate's tricks, always in a rush,
Yet pause for a snack, amid the chaotic hush.

Like cats with their yarn, we dance and play,
Finding joy in the mess that brightens our day.
If plans go awry, we adopt a new tune,
Chasing butterflies under a silly, bright moon.

With socks mismatched, we strut our style,
Embracing the madness, all the while.
In the symphony of blunders, we sing out loud,
Celebrating the chaos, both silly and proud.

Reflections in a Cracked Mirror

Gazing at myself in a warped glass frame,
I chuckle at features that seem quite the same.
Each crack tells a tale of my wild escapades,
Where laughter and puzzlement always invade.

In this funhouse of thoughts, I twirl and flip,
My quirky reflections taking a dip.
With every odd angle, a grin shows its face,
Life's just a circus, and I enjoy the chase.

Is that really me? Oh, what a sight!
With hair like a tumbleweed, laughter feels right.
Each time I trip over thoughts on the floor,
I stumble but chuckle and look for more.

Seasons of the Soul

Spring brings the glee, with blossoms in bloom,
But summer's so hot, it can feel like a sauna room.
Autumn whispers laughter in leaves painted gold,
While winter arrives, with stories untold.

We dance through the seasons, like leaves on the breeze,
Collecting odd moments that aim to please.
With scarves and mittens, we frolic and play,
Life's a peculiar party, come join the fray!

Seasonal changes bring quirks to each day,
From floating like snowflakes to sunburned ballet.
Every twist and turn, we find our own role,
In this whimsical journey, we savor our soul.

A Maze of Questions

Here I am again, lost in my thought maze,
Asking if coffee counts as a healthy phase.
Why do ducks quack? Is spaghetti a friend?
In this puzzle of ponderings, where does it end?

Each question a riddle, a giggle, a grin,
Do fish get thirsty, or do they just swim?
With curiosity bouncing like a bouncing ball,
We stumble through queries while having a ball.

Like a cat with a laser, I chase after why,
Questioning existence beneath the vast sky.
With laughter as compass, my thoughts take a spin,
In this maze of conundrums, the fun's where we begin!

Unveiling the Masks We Wear

In a world full of faces,
We juggle all our roles,
Clowning through life's mazes,
Chasing after goals.

With wigs and silly shoes,
We dance like it's a game,
As laughter drowns the blues,
Even when it's the same.

Behind each painted smile,
Is chaos we can't hide,
Yet we flaunt our style,
In this wild joyride.

So cast away your fears,
Let's toast to midnight schemes,
We'll snicker through the years,
And weave absurdist dreams.

The Beauty of Uneven Paths

Steps that twist and stumble,
Lead us to strange places,
Life's truly quite a jumble,
Full of unexpected graces.

With every wrong turn taken,
We find a new delight,
Our plans may often be shaken,
But laughter feels so right.

Rocks might bruise our toes,
And puddles soak our socks,
Yet every laugh that flows,
Is worth a hundred knocks.

Embrace the quirky bends,
For they teach us to roam,
In the mess, joy transcends,
And our hearts find their home.

Singing to the Moon's Shadow

With a moonlit serenade,
We croon to the night sky,
Frogs join in the parade,
While stars blink shy goodbye.

Oh, how we sing so loud,
To echoes and some quirks,
Dancing like a proud crowd,
Creating joyful smirks.

The moon grins down with glee,
At our off-key charade,
Life's a whimsical spree,
A wild, cosmic charade.

So let's howl at the sky,
In harmony, we thrive,
Laughing as we fly high,
In this jumbled life hive.

A Quest for the Unfathomable

We set forth on a search,
For wisdom on a whim,
Holding tight to our perch,
While moments start to swim.

With maps drawn by the clueless,
And riddles wrapped in jokes,
Our wisdom feels quite lossy,
Like fishing for mere blokes.

We question why we're here,
With munchies on our quest,
As giggles drown our fear,
And nonsense feels the best.

So let the journey wend,
Though answers may elude,
We'll laugh with every bend,
And find joy in the brood.

Understanding Through Curiosity

Why do ducks quack in the park?
Is it deep? Is it spark?
Life's a puzzle with missing pieces,
Where sense and nonsense often ceases.

Einstein said, 'E=mc^2',
Is that when a cow becomes a sphere?
Questions tumble like sock puppets,
In a world that spins and then erupts.

A bouncing ball rolls down the street,
Chasing shadows on two left feet.
In search of wisdom, what a laugh!
Digesting thoughts like a giant giraffe.

With each 'why' more chaos takes flight,
Curiosity keeps us up at night.
To decipher life's quirky layers,
Ask a cat; it knows the players.

Where Silence Speaks Volumes

Do you hear that? It's quite loud,
Silence stands strong, like a crowd.
It whispers secrets, oh so sly,
Like a cat plotting for a pie.

Sometimes silence leans on a chair,
Stares at you with a curious glare.
Is it judging or just daydreaming?
It's hard to say when the clock is beaming.

In awkward moments, it makes a scene,
Where conversations become just routine.
A mime with passion, no words to share,
Yet lifts the veil of the everyday air.

So cherish the quiet; it's a dance,
A pause in the chatter, a cosmic chance.
In the hush, reflections reveal,
The funniest truths and how we feel.

The Art of Lost Connections

Once I lost my keys and my mind,
Where did they go? One of a kind!
Connection's a game of hide and seek,
With socks that vanish and chairs that creak.

Texting my cat, got no reply,
She's too busy plotting as I sigh.
The art of connection's a tangled thread,
Where I find meanings in what's unsaid.

Neighbors wave but can't recall names,
They talk of weather, play small-talking games.
Are we all stars in a cosmic play?
Making sure we don't drift away.

In the chaos, we try to relate,
Navigating life like a blind date.
Lost connections, they trail behind,
Funny how we get so intertwined.

Evaporating into the Infinite

Watch a balloon slowly take flight,
Evaporating with sheer delight.
Up it goes, with a giggle and grin,
Life's a carnival, let the fun begin!

How does a cloud hold raindrop shows?
Does it tickle the sky with its whimsical prose?
Floating freely, it sometimes drags,
The soul's essence in shimmering rags.

Infinity's just a big, messy game,
Where socks and dreams go up in flames.
Laugh as you drift on the cosmic breeze,
For the answer is hidden in gentle tease.

So dance with the stars, skip on the sun,
Evaporate slowly, it's all about fun!
Let go of worries, embrace the sky,
And remember, it's okay to float by.

Unwinding the Fabric of Now

Thread by thread, we pull at fate,
Hoping for a simple date.
Yet every twist, a tangled line,
We laugh as chaos stands in line.

Life's like knitting with no end,
A ball of yarn, around we bend.
With needles crossed, we take a chance,
In every stitch, we find a dance.

Plotting paths like a hedgehog's quest,
Searching deep for humor's zest.
Curling ideas, who knows if they'll stay?
A sweater woven, worn, and frayed.

Unravel dreams, let laughter lead,
With every knot, we plant a seed.
Life's a fabric, mismatched but bright,
Stitched together, oh what a sight!

A Symphony of Silent Sighs

In the orchestra of daily grind,
Silent sighs and laughs combined.
A clash of pots, a cheerful crash,
Life's a concert, not a bash.

The conductor waves, we fumble tune,
Singing loudly beneath the moon.
Yet every note resolves in cheer,
Frustration's symphony, oh so dear.

A waltz with worries, toes entwined,
In rhythm with the curious mind.
Offbeat laughter, it's all the craze,
Dancing through life's quirky maze.

So gather round, with friends, we try,
To find the joy in every sigh.
For in the music, sweet and spry,
We hum our truths, let laughter fly.

The Weight of Unanswered Prayers

We toss our hopes like paper planes,
Yet most of them just fly in vain.
A prayer for snacks, or sunny skies,
Turns into a cosmic surprise.

With unanswered wishes piled high,
We wonder if there's a reason why.
Did the universe misread the card?
Or play a joke? Oh, life's so hard!

Each heavy thought, a feather's weight,
We ponder what might have been fate.
At times despair, then brittle cheer,
In awkward silence, cries appear.

We laugh in the midst of our plight,
Finding joy in the absurdity of night.
With heavy hearts, we sail away,
On waves of laughter, come what may.

Wandering Through the Maze of Time

Lost in clocks that tick and tock,
Feeling like an old cuckoo clock.
Step by step, we wander free,
Through the corridors of mystery.

Each twist and turn, a puzzled face,
Running laps in a timeless race.
Fumbling dates as seconds fly,
With every moment, a silly sigh.

Yet through the maze, we trip and fall,
Finding joy in the grand hall.
Chasing shadows, laughing loud,
In the chaos, we're beautifully proud.

So grab a friend, let's share the ride,
What wonders wait, we can't decide.
Though time's a prankster, let's not fret,
We'll dance through mazes we never met!

Journey through the Labyrinth

In a maze of dreams we roam,
Searching for a place called home.
Every turn is full of quirks,
Nonsense hides where logic lurks.

Maps are drawn in spaghetti lines,
Lost again, but hey, that shines!
With laughter echoing through the halls,
We trip on fate and bounce off walls.

Each corner turned, a riddle waits,
We chuckle as confusion fates.
Do we have the answer? Maybe not!
But isn't that the funniest plot?

In this whirlwind, we find delight,
As we dance in the soft twilight.
Life's a twisty, topsy game,
And who needs sense when you've got fame?

Embraced by the Unknown

Here we stand, arms open wide,
To the mystery that we can't hide.
Whispers tease us, calling near,
With jokes from things we hold most dear.

Wrapped in blankets of doubt and cheer,
We sip on chai while spinning here.
What if the signal is just noise?
Let's search for bliss, not static poise.

Stars giggle down from their great heights,
Making fun of our sleepless nights.
We chase what seems a wild goose,
But giggles are our secret juice.

In shadows cast by our own fears,
We find the courage wrapped in cheers.
Embrace the joke, the cosmic jest,
For laughter's truly the very best.

Unraveling the Paradox

In a world where nothing's clear,
We unravel knots, we shed a tear.
Logic laughs as feelings fight,
It's a waltz of wrong and right.

To be or not, who can decide?
Yet here we are, with arms spread wide.
The paradox sits on the couch,
Cracking jokes, oh what a slouch!

Answers dance like lightning bugs,
While we stumble through warm hugs.
Each contradiction brings a grin,
As we embrace the chaos within.

So let's toast to the tangled mess,
Finding humor in this process.
For twists and turns make it grand,
And laughter is our guiding hand.

Chasing Shadows and Light

We chase the shadows, run and twist,
In search of what we can't resist.
Light feels heavy, shadows sing,
What's the point of this whole fling?

Flashlight in hand, we laugh and play,
As flickers dance and tease the fray.
In shadows deep, we find our spark,
Creating joy within the dark.

Life's a blend of shades and tones,
In every laugh, a truth is sown.
Yet when we stumble and it feels odd,
We just giggle and give a nod.

So here's to shadows and playful light,
With each riddle, we take flight.
In the chase of all that's bright,
We discover joy, our true insight.

Awakening to Ambiguity.

Woke up this morning, who am I today?
Coffee in hand, in a puzzling ballet.
Socks mismatched, oh what a sight,
Life's a circus, not black and white.

Float through the day, like a butterfly,
Chasing my thoughts, just passing by.
What's art? What's life? Who cares to define?
Just keep dancing, and sip your wine.

Questions arise like popcorn in a pan,
Why do I exist? Say what you can!
With a chuckle, I shrug it off tight,
Laughter is wisdom, and it feels just right.

At night, I ponder, let my thoughts roam,
Is happiness real, or a glittering foam?
In the end, who really has the clue?
Let's just laugh and enjoy the view!

Winding Roads of Existence

Driving in circles, where am I bound?
GPS says left but right's all around.
Life's a maze with a sign that says, "Detour!"
For every wrong turn, there's a little more bore.

Step on the gas, then hit the brakes,
Reality's a puzzle, full of high stakes.
Should I stop for ice cream or chase big dreams?
Just follow your nose, nothing's as it seems.

Talking to squirrels, they nod and agree,
What's the secret to being carefree?
They chatter away, no worries in mind,
Like fluffy therapists, they're one of a kind.

So let's hit the road, with snacks in the back,
Whether we're lost or just off the track,
Every giggle and twist, a story to share,
Life's a wild ride, just handle with care!

Shadows in a Glass House

In a house made of windows, I dance with the light,
Shadows play games, a delight in the night.
I caught one whisper, it tickled my ear,
Life's a riddle wrapped up in cheer.

Reflecting my thoughts, like a funhouse mirror,
Sometimes I'm tall, and sometimes I'm nearer.
What's real? What's fake? It's all such a show,
I laugh at the shape of the things that I know.

Curious critters peek through the glass,
Judging my life, as they strut and sass.
I raise my cup, to my ghostly friends,
No need for an answer, just droll amends.

Throw wisdom to the wind, let's play in the rain,
Escape from the norms, refuse to explain.
In a glass house of shadows, we giggle with glee,
The trick to it all? Just let it be free!

Echoes of Unasked Questions

In a room full of whispers, I hear the unknown,
Questions that linger, but seldom are shown.
Why is the sky so ridiculously blue?
And why are my shoes always stuck to the glue?

Pondering pancakes and syrupy dreams,
Are we just atoms in whimsical schemes?
Juggling the why's with a side of the how,
Life's a talent show, who gets the bow?

The truth is a riddle, a jesting friend,
It makes you laugh, but you can't comprehend.
So let's pop the confetti, and twirl all around,
For life is a dance, in joy we are bound.

So throw up your hands, with no need for a plan,
Life's a messy feast, come join if you can!
In echoes of questions, we stumble and sway,
Finding the funny in every cliché!

Navigating The River of Chance

In a boat made of dreams, we float,
Sipping tea with a talking goat.
Rocks and whirlpools, oh what a ride,
With humor as our trusted guide.

Fish that wear hats swim on by,
They wink and quack, oh my, oh my!
Every wave a riddle, every splash a joke,
In this crazy river, we simply provoke.

A captain with socks mismatched,
Navigates paths he's yet to hatch.
Yet laughter fills the air so bright,
With each twist and turn, it feels just right.

Life's just a party on this tidal wave,
Each moment a chance, be bold and brave!
Let's dance with the currents, twist and spin,
For fortune favors those with a grin!

Portraits of the Unseen

In the attic of thoughts, dust bunnies reign,
Each one a tale, a joy, or a pain.
They whisper secrets of days gone past,
Yet some hang around, just having a blast.

A cat with a monocle, painting a scene,
While a cabbage in glasses pretends to be keen.
Life's an art gallery full of surprise,
Where even the mundane wears a disguise.

A chair claims it's wise, an old rug feels grand,
As soap suds emerge from a bar of soap's hand.
They chat about purpose, and the space in between,
As laughter erupts over things unforeseen.

What speaks to the heart, what tickles the mind?
A jester in shadows, it's all intertwined.
These portraits of moments, both silly and deep,
In the hall of existence, we chuckle, we leap!

Embracing Complexity: A Clay Pot

A potter molds clay with unmatched flair,
Shaping our quirks—with love and care.
Its curves tell of chaos, its dents hold a laugh,
In the wobbliness dwells the true craft.

Oh look, it spills tea with a cheeky grin,
While gossiping warmly with the spoon and the tin.
Life's just a vessel for stories untold,
Each crack like a memory, a glimpse of gold.

Embracing our flaws, the pot sings a tune,
With spatters of paint, and moonlight so strewn.
It dances on shelves, proudly adorned,
Reminding us all, the best days are worn.

So let's toast to the pot, let's raise a cheer,
For all of the mess and the joy that we steer!
In every misstep, a treasure we find,
In this glorious chaos, we're joyfully blind!

Tumbling in the Circles of Existence

Round and round in the cosmic dance,
We chase our tails in a whimsical trance.
A hamster on wheels, so wild and free,
With popcorn and laughter, we make quite a spree.

Elves in the corners, they giggle and cheer,
As penguins in bowties slyly appear.
Each loop that we take spins stories anew,
The universe winks—it's all just a view.

Chasing our shadows, we bounce off the walls,
Finding the joy in the rise and the falls.
A ball pit of moments, soft yet profound,
In spirals of laughter, true fun can be found.

So let's twirl in the circles, embrace the delight,
In the circus of living, we shine ever bright!
With friends by our side, there's nothing to fear,
Just tumbling together, let's drink in the cheer!

The Dance of Questions Unasked

Why is the sky so blue and wide?
Do ducks believe they can fly with pride?
Is coffee a hug in a steaming cup?
Or just a trick to wake me up?

I ponder if socks have feelings too,
When lost, do they cry, or search for a shoe?
Why do we laugh at our own tall tales?
Is life just a game of wondrous scales?

What if balloons could speak their mind?
Would they tell secrets, truthfully blind?
Do stars peek down to see our fate?
Or are they just twinkling out of date?

So here I tiptoe on thoughts a'plenty,
Wrapped in giggles, slightly unbendy.
In a universe vast and a little absurd,
We dance on questions that seem unheard.

Traces of Yesterday's Sunrise

The morning light spills like melted cheese,
Whispers of yesterday carried by the breeze.
Why do we cherish the light and the dark?
Perhaps it all starts with a simple spark.

Pancakes flipped with a dash of hope,
Do they dream of syrup or learn how to cope?
As toast pops up, is it feeling grand?
Or wishing for butter to lend a hand?

Do shadows giggle as day turns to night?
Are they just playing in the fading light?
If clocks could tick with a sense of flair,
Would they synchronize just to show they care?

Yet here we sit, mugs in hand,
Wondering how time slipped right through our sand.
In laughter we find the day's little fables,
As we ponder life over brunch at the tables.

Weaving Wondrous Whys

In the garden of queries, seeds are sown,
Each petal a question, fully grown.
What's with the turtles and their slow grind?
Do they work harder in search of the mind?

Is chocolate a fruit, or just a sweet game?
Perhaps it's a riddle dressed up with fame.
What if clouds are just pillows of dreams?
Floating about in whimsical streams?

What does the rooster say at dawn?
Is he announcing a new day we've drawn?
Are ants in a hurry or just on a spree?
Bound to their purpose, as busy can be?

Through tangled thoughts we frolic and play,
Chasing the wisdom that skips on the way.
In laughter and joy, we find our delight,
In weaving our whys through day and night.

Blossoms of Uncertainty

In a field where wild questions bloom,
Answers flutter about like a broom.
Why do we fear the unknown so much?
Is it the thrill or a bit of a crutch?

If cats have nine lives, what's the end game?
A career in acting or a patch of fame?
Do they giggle at humans running around?
Or just plot their next leap from the ground?

Why do we dance when the music is right?
Is it joy, or a way to take flight?
What if laughter is just our own spark?
Guiding us lovingly through the dark?

So embrace these blossoms, both wobbly and bright,
For in their petals, we find our light.
Through questions unchained, we twirl and we laugh,
Finding joy in the riddles, our own little path.

Kaleidoscope of Hopes and Fears

In a dance of dreams we prance,
Chasing colors in a trance.
Fear's a clown with painted cheer,
While hope's a jester drawing near.

Twists and turns of fate's delight,
Sometimes wrong, yet feels so right.
Hopes collide with fears so grand,
In this wacky wonderland.

Life's a mix of sweet and sour,
An hourglass, a fleeting hour.
We juggle thoughts that tease and taunt,
And laugh at what we cannot flaunt.

So join the show, don't grip too tight,
In this carnival of spite.
Let's bloom and wilt, but still aspire,
To swim through joy and laugh in fire.

The Paradox of Yesterdays

Yesterday's an old-time fool,
Lessons learned, but still we drool.
On what was said or left unsaid,
Like dropping toast, we land on bread.

Memories haunt like pesky flies,
Buzzing loud with forgotten cries.
Regrets parade in silly hats,
While laughter gives the dogs their pats.

Oh, to ponder the should-have-beens,
Drowning in our might-have-seens.
Time's a trickster, pulls the strings,
As we chase dreams like bouncy springs.

Let's dance with ghosts, but not too close,
In the land of what matters most.
For every fumble's but a quirk,
In life's grand play, we all must twerk.

Embracing the Unknown

What's behind that curtain there?
A monster or a teddy bear?
Life's a mystery, with laughs and shrieks,
Holding secrets in wanders and leaks.

We dressed in doubt, wore silly hats,
And wrestled with our own mishaps.
Curiosity's a playful pup,
Chasing tails while we cheer it up.

Dare to peek beyond the door,
The world outside says, "Here's more!"
With every step, we waddle blind,
Yet find delights, treasures to unwind.

So let's embrace the twisted roads,
With smirks and giggles, let's unload.
For in the fear of what's to come,
Is where the zaniest joy is from.

Harmonies of Dissonance

Life's a song of offbeat tunes,
Sung by cats beneath the moons.
A choir of quirks in harmony,
Revving chaos like a symphony.

Up and down, the notes collide,
Dissonance is where we bide.
We tap our feet to awkward beats,
In a world where nonsense greets.

The rhythm shifts, we swing and sway,
With giggles marking every stray.
So hum along, don't miss the beat,
In this eccentric, quirky feat.

Let laughter fill the silent gaps,
As life spins circles, twists like chaps.
For in the discord, joy abounds,
A wacky song that knows no bounds.

Chasing Fleeting Whispers

In a world of endless chatter,
We all seek the hidden patter.
Finding answers in a riddle,
Laughing as we play the fiddle.

Running after fleeting dreams,
Like chasing shadows, or so it seems.
With every twist and turn we take,
We stumble, giggle, and then we break.

In this search for something grand,
We trip and fall, make silly plans.
The more we look, the less we find,
Smiling at the tricks of mind.

What's out there, is it all for show?
A cosmic joke, or just for fun, you know?
So we dance through this absurd charade,
With a wink and nod, our fears allayed.

Dance of the Uncertain Heart

Oh, what a jig the heart will play,
With every thump, it finds a way.
Two steps forward, then a slide,
Twisting tales like a rollercoaster ride.

In a room filled with lovesick sighs,
The choices whirl like butterflies.
Do I choose the sweet or sour?
All that glitters loses power.

The heart is bold, but also shy,
It flutters, ponders, oh my, oh my!
In laughter and in awkward grace,
It stumbles through this dance of fate.

So let's embrace this wobbly waltz,
With silly moves that have no faults.
Together we'll make clumsy art,
In the dance of the uncertain heart.

Threads of Destiny Unraveled

Life's a tapestry, bright and bold,
With threads that twist and stories told.
One wrong pull, and chaos reigns,
As we laugh at our tangled chains.

A thread of gold, a thread of doubt,
We yank and tug, we laugh and shout.
Trying to weave a grander plan,
But all we've got is a tiny yarn strand.

Each knot we make, a moment Grey,
Pull tighter and watch our troubles sway.
Yet in this mess, a pattern remains,
A chaotic dance, through joys and pains.

So let's embrace our frayed design,
With silly grins and glasses of wine.
For every twist life throws our way,
It's all part of this fabric play.

Labyrinths of Thought

In the maze of what we think we know,
We wander aimlessly, to and fro.
Each corner turned reveals a clue,
But then, which path should we pursue?

Thoughts collide in frantic cheer,
Whispers echo, insights clear.
Lost in questions, we scratch our heads,
All the while, laughing, "What's with the threads?"

Through recesses of the mind we skip,
Falling down every rabbit trip.
The answers hide in playful jest,
As we ponder what's truly best.

So grab a friend and lose your way,
In this labyrinth of thoughts we play.
For tangled thoughts can bring delight,
Even in the strange afterthoughts at night.

Melodies of Existential Wonders

In a world so wide, we still lose our keys,
Searching high and low, while swatting at bees.
Life's a quirky tune, sometimes offbeat,
Dancing through doubts with two left feet.

What's the purpose, we ask with a sigh,
As we trip on our shoelaces and slyly cry.
We ponder and giggle, in a comic display,
For some answers, we find, just slip away.

Chasing big dreams while we munch on some pie,
Asking the universe: 'Oh, who am I?'
Each twist and turn, a laugh or a fall,
Maybe the answer's just to have a ball.

So let's toast to questions and uncertain signs,
With laughter that bubbles like good vintage wines.
For life's a riddle wrapped in a jest,
And joy, my dear friends, is truly the best.

A Dance with Destiny

In the grand ballroom, where fate takes a spin,
I stepped on the toes of a fate I can't win.
Each twirl and each dip, a graceful charade,
With a partner named 'Chaos' who never obeyed.

Destiny chuckles as I trip on my lace,
A dance floor of mishaps, a spectacular space.
I'll tango with time, and hop with delight,
Where confusion is sparkly and wrong feels so right.

Every misstep is simply a beat,
With life's disco ball shining bright in the heat.
The music may falter, but I'll take the chance,
And laugh through the nonsense, while I lose my pants.

So here's to the rhythm of life's wild embrace,
To frolic with fate like it's a silly race.
Because amidst the laughter and confusion we find,
There's humor in life that's brilliantly blind.

Secrets of the Unseen

Behind every curtain of mystery's sheen,
Are socks that get lost and moments unseen.
Like dodging a question that's bound to perplex,
While giggling at chaos that's simply complex.

We consult all the oracles, wise and absurd,
While pondering things that we've never quite heard.
With a wink and a nod to the universe wide,
Where where's and why's turn into a ride.

The greatest of truths? Just enjoy the ride,
As we float down the river with errors as guide.
From serious moments to laughs that collide,
There's laughter in secrets that hope will confide.

So let's raise our glasses to moments that gleam,
To the funny side of our puzzling theme.
For deep in the chaos, a chuckle's the key,
Unlocking the laughter in life's great mystery.

Beyond the Veil of Time

In the realm of the timeless, with food off a shelf,
I wonder, just where did I leave my other self?
A glitch in the matrix, or perhaps it's my hair,
Time travels with laughter, just handle with care.

We whirl through the epochs like socks in the wash,
Trying to catch wisdom with too much panache.
Each second a riddle, a bubble that pops,
As we navigate moments like clowns in flip-flops.

Future's a puzzle, past is a joke,
Full of inside gags and half-baked smoke.
Laugh lines will fade, yet wisdom will bloom,
As we sidestep the doubts while we shuffle the room.

So let's giggle through time, and toast to the jest,
To the wacky adventures, and life's funny quest.
For in all of the moments that twist and unwind,
The joy in the journey is a treasure to find.

Chasing the Sunbeam's Edge

In a world of glitter and glee,
We stumble through the entropy.
Chasing sunbeams, we trip and fall,
Is this wisdom or nonsense at all?

We juggle dreams like hot potatoes,
And laugh at life's quirky interpreters.
With each slip, we find delight,
Like cats in shoes at midnight.

Who needs a map with a chart?
We venture forth with a goofy start.
Each laughter echoes, a joyous song,
Even if our path feels wrong.

So tip your hat to the fleeting haze,
And dance through life's ridiculous maze.
With sunflowers sprouting from our heads,
We toast to adventures, not to dreads!

Secrets Beneath the Skin

Beneath the surface, we all are clowns,
With painted smiles and goofy frowns.
Finding truths in the most odd places,
Like socks that hide and steal our laces.

We ponder fate while eating cake,
Each layer thick, a fun mistake.
Wrapped in laughter, we dive right in,
Contemplating where we've been and been.

Life's an enigma, a wild surprise,
Like trying to guess a puppy's size.
In the chaos, we manage to grin,
Finding joy in secrets beneath our skin.

We're quirky, we're weird, we've got tales to tell,
In a world where all's kooky, we may fit quite well.
So chuckle and giggle, don't take it too fast,
In this carnival of life, enjoy the blast!

Dances of Duality

In a tale of two, we weave and sigh,
With ups and downs like a roller fly.
We flip the coin; it's heads, it's tails,
A merry-go-round of whimsy trails.

The sun and the moon share a quirky dance,
They spin through trouble, they twirl in chance.
Even shadows join in the fun,
Competing for laughs till the day is done.

Life's a jigsaw with pieces misplaced,
Sometimes we trip, sometimes we're graced.
With every twirl, we find our way,
In laughter's arms, we choose to stay.

So join the parade with snacks to munch,
As life does its dance, let's take a punch.
With rhythm and rhyme, we'll sway all night,
In this playful duel, everything feels right!

Flickers of Light in Dark Corners

In the shadows where secrets lie,
Flickers of light make spirits fly.
With mismatched socks and twinkling toes,
We find our joy where nobody knows.

Clumsy steps lead to hidden rewards,
Like discovering treasure without any swords.
Each chuckle hides a flicker or two,
In the chaos, we find something new.

We dance with lights, we kick at the gloom,
Shaking our fists at worries that loom.
With every giggle, the dark fades away,
In our silly circus, we choose to play.

So let laughter echo in shadowy rooms,
And let our joy blossom like wild blooms.
For in the flickers, the strange truths unfurl,
That life's a laugh — oh, what a whirl!

When Clouds Weep Rainbows

Clouds above, a weepy sight,
They've lost their way, so sad, so light.
But watch them dance, a quirky show,
A colorful splash, a jovial glow.

Puddles form, they start to play,
Jumping in, who needs a bouquet?
Laughter rings in the dreamy rain,
Life's a game, embrace the absurd pain.

A rainbow's grin, delights the eyes,
While ducks waddle by in fancy ties.
With every drop, we find our cheer,
Oh, the joy in life's wet veneer!

So let the storms come, we'll make a splash,
As we dance through puddles, quick and brash.
With each whimsy, we create our art,
In the world's canvas, we play our part.

Fragments of a Jigsaw Soul

A puzzle piece without a frame,
Confused and lost, but not to blame.
Searching for corners, edges, and lines,
In this game of life, we're all designs.

Some fit here, some fit there,
Yet still we laugh, with wild flair.
No picture clear, it's all a mess,
But isn't chaos just the best?

I'm a cat at play, with yarn in tow,
Tangled by fate, oh where to go?
Every twist, a brand-new laugh,
Finding joy in the aftermath!

So grab your pieces, let's make it bright,
In colorful patches, life takes flight.
We'll create a scene that breaks the mold,
In this jigsaw game, daring and bold.

Silent Stories of Our Being

Whispers float in the midnight air,
Tales untold, we choose to share.
Life's a comedian, a jesting bard,
In silence, it's never too hard.

Giggling stars, winking with glee,
As we share secrets, just you and me.
The moon chuckles, casting its light,
"Oh dear, humans, what a silly sight!"

Footsteps echo on the cosmic floor,
A waltz with fate, always wanting more.
Dancing shadows, spinning round,
In each quiet moment, laughter found.

So let's sing softly, under the skies,
With snickers and giggles, let's be wise.
For in the silence, stories unfold,
The tales of our lives glimmer like gold.

Beneath the Surface of Simplicity

Under layers of everyday cheer,
Lies a riddle, a puzzling sphere.
We sip our tea, nod with a smile,
What's hiding beneath? Just a quirky style!

A tune plays softly, oh what's that beat?
The dance of socks that went off their feet.
In mundane moments, joy can arise,
It tickles us pink, a sweet surprise!

Life is a game of peek-a-boo,
Where simplicity hides something new.
So let's dig deep, unearth the fun,
In the ordinary, we'll never be done!

Beneath the calm, there swirls a spree,
Of quirky laughter, wild and free.
In every heartbeat, a fun little twist,
Oh, let's embrace it, we cannot resist!

Fables Born from Shadows

In shadows, tales begin to weave,
With quirks and quirks, they never leave.
A cat in boots, a duck that sings,
Life's a circus with crazy flings.

Lost socks dance in the echoing dark,
A squirrel claims his secret park.
Bananas ride on zebras' backs,
They whisper truths while hiding tracks.

Mice wear glasses, wise and bold,
Telling secrets that never get old.
The world spins wildly, round and round,
In laughter's grip, our woes are drowned.

Dreams are like piñatas, hanging high,
Smash them open, let candy fly.
Life's odd riddles, a puzzle we make,
In giggles and grins, we share the break.

Whispers of Forgotten Memories

Once I lost my shoes on street,
Turns out they danced to a funky beat.
A frog in a tux, my old friend dear,
Said, "Life's a party, let's raise a cheer!"

My diary spills tales of old,
Of ice-cream sundaes and friends so bold.
Each page a mishap, a funny plight,
Spaghetti fights under the moonlight.

A cat that knits with yarn so bright,
Recites the ponderings of day and night.
With every stitch, a secret's sewn,
In laughter's echo, we're never alone.

As twilight hums its sleepy tune,
Joy floats gently like a balloon.
In whispers soft, we reminisce,
Life's comedy, a quirky bliss.

A Tapestry of Daring Journeys

A hedgehog with a map and flair,
Sets off to find rare stardust air.
With every step, his quills shake free,
Plot twists waiting 'neath the old oak tree.

In search of treasures, both odd and rare,
Unicorns giggle, float without a care.
A penguin in boots leads the parade,
Through marshmallow fields, memories fade.

Life's a scavenger hunt, a quirky quest,
With puzzles solved and spontaneous jest.
Kites made of jelly, flying high,
Scarves of whimsy draped in the sky.

Each fork in the road a chance to play,
With every misstep, we dance and sway.
In the tapestry woven, laughs intertwine,
Adventures await, you'll be just fine.

Mandalas of Our Inner Worlds

In mandalas spun with giggles tight,
Colors burst forth, a joyful sight.
A monkey in shades joins the parade,
With crazy antics, he's never afraid.

We doodle dreams on the canvas of time,
Sprinkled with laughter, a steady climb.
Pet goldfish wearing tiny hats,
Dance on the tables, oh how it spats!

A world where logic takes a break,
Where jellybeans are the things we bake.
Each swirl and twirl, a story made,
In the maze of fun, our hearts cascade.

So grab your crayons, let's play pretend,
In mandalas vast, let joy transcend.
For in this universe, wild and dear,
We find ourselves, and that's the cheer.

Voids That Shape Our Dreams

In the dance of empty chairs,
We ponder with empty stares.
Life's a puzzle with missing cords,
As we juggle dreams with broken swords.

A trampoline for thoughts that flop,
Bouncing high till we just drop.
Questions swirl in peanut butter,
With sighs so loud, our hearts just stutter.

Laughter echoes like a ghost,
Chasing dreams we love the most.
In holes of logic, we might trip,
But smile wide, and take a sip.

Stars above with winks so sly,
Remind us of the reason why.
In every void, there's room to play,
Life's a game, hip-hip-hooray!

Seasons of the Soul

Winter's chill wraps us tight,
Yet we wear shorts, what a sight!
Spring brings confusion in full bloom,
While summer roasts and makes us fume.

Autumn leaves dance like crazy fools,
While we question all the rules.
In seasonal shifts, we laugh and sweat,
With socks on hands, never forget!

Time's a jester with a grin,
Dressing us in mismatched skin.
Each season's tricks keep us awake,
Like ice cream scoops in a cake.

We try to read the leaves and skies,
But nature's riddles don't comply.
Through every change, we find delight,
With chuckles soft in day and night.

Reflections in a Crystal Sphere

In a glass ball, the truth appears,
With visions swirled between our cheers.
We peek inside, but it's a jest,
Like looking at life in a funny vest.

Mirrors whisper secret tales,
As we trip on our own trails.
What's the wisdom of the sphere?
Just more fun, and frothy beer!

Warped perceptions make us giggle,
Like squishy jelly in a wiggle.
Every glance, a riddle spun,
Life's a circus, and we're the fun.

So here we gleam, and here we jest,
In crystal truths, we find our quest.
With blurry edges, dreams reprieve,
Laugh a bit, and then believe!

Labors of Love and Loss

Love's a job that pays in hugs,
But comes with an army of pesky bugs.
We toil with hopes both grand and small,
Like knitting sweaters with spaghetti, y'all.

Loss tosses us like a game of catch,
In a field where emotions scratch.
We sweep the past with a silly broom,
And dance in chaos, making room.

Yet in this work, we find the fun,
Like baking pies with cherries none.
Through all the trials, we'll always cheer,
With jokes that stick like glue, my dear.

So raise a glass, let laughter flow,
For love and loss both steal the show.
In burdens shared, we find our bliss,
In the hug of life, a sweet, warm kiss.

Poems from the Edge of Chaos

In the fridge, a monster looms,
Leftovers dance in endless glooms.
Life's a party, but where's the cake?
I swear I saw it, for goodness' sake!

We juggle dreams like circus clowns,
With mighty hopes and silly frowns.
But when the music starts to fade,
Do we waltz, or do we trade?

A cat strolls by, so full of pride,
While we're lost in life's chaotic ride.
An ice cream cone, the value's clear,
But is it fleeting, or will it adhere?

So laugh with me, in all this mess,
For in the chaos, we find our zest.
Throw your worries into the fray,
In this wild game, we'll find our way!

Moments Suspended in Time

A clock ticks loud, yet feels so still,
In moments lost, we find the thrill.
Like socks unmatched after the wash,
A puzzle missing pieces - oh what a nosh!

We chase our tails like anxious hounds,
In endless loops of silly rounds.
With every giggle, wisdom slips,
Could time be measured in silly quips?

A cup of tea, a splash of glee,
Each sip's a chance for jubilee.
So let's toast to time's amusing dance,
In mismatched shoes, we'll take our chance!

When seconds stretch and moments pause,
Let's revel in life's funny laws.
For in these quirks, we find our rhyme,
Lost in laughter, we conquer time!

Treading the Tightrope of Truth

We walk a line so thin and taut,
With balance found in what we sought.
A truth that wiggles, makes us sway,
Like a tightrope act on a sunny day!

With facts and fiction, we twist and turn,
In this grand circus, we live and learn.
Did I drop my keys or change my mind?
In this wild ride, what will we find?

Truths wrapped in riddles, we laugh so loud,
A family portrait, so far from proud.
But in the giggles, we find our way,
Treading the line, come what may!

So grab some cotton candy, dear friend,
Let's celebrate how we twist and bend.
In this funhouse mirror, we see anew,
The tightrope of truth, just me and you!

Moons in a Sunlit Sky

When the sun shines bright, the moon chuckles,
Hiding behind clouds, performing snuggles.
Life's a stage with shifting scenes,
Where laughter lurks in daily routines.

Like a goldfish dreaming in a bowl,
We ponder big things, while snacks take a toll.
Between the bites and giggles shared,
We ponder questions we haven't dared.

The moon whispers secrets of cosmic delight,
While we're busy searching for lost socks at night.
In wacky thoughts, we find our bliss,
Life's puzzle pieces often go amiss.

So dance with shadows in all their grace,
Embrace the silliness of our space.
In moons that glow in sunlit skies,
We'll laugh so hard, we might just fly!

Whispers in the Infinite

In the café of time, we sip and sigh,
What's the secret? Oh, we just don't know why!
Between laughs and worries, we lose the plot,
Hoping the universe has a great big shot.

Beneath the surface, the chaos flows,
Like a sock in the wash, where no one knows.
We dance through confusion, a comical spree,
Who thought existence would come with a fee?

Questions emerge, each stranger than twine,
As we twirl in our chairs, sipping cheap wine.
Life's a bizarre game, with rules that are bent,
And the scoreboard is blank, what a time we've spent!

So let's raise a toast to the wobbly road,
For in laughter and chaos, we lighten the load.
With giggles and grumbles, we'll figure it out,
Or just kick back and enjoy the clout!

Threads of Existence

Weaving and stitching, life's such a mess,
Like mismatched socks, can't you guess?
Each thread tells a story, some sad, some bright,
In the fabric of being, we dance through the night.

Like a cat on a rug, we tumble and sway,
As questions arise in the strangest way.
Do we chase after answers or just grab a snack?
With popcorn and giggles, we'll find the right track!

Moments like puzzles, some weird and some fun,
Trying to fit pieces that never quite run.
So we laugh at the chaos, embrace it with glee,
Life's a quirky adventure, let's all agree!

So come take my hand, let's twist and unwind,
In this wobbly journey, we'll see what we find.
With joy and confusion, we'll strut down the street,
For the threads of existence are utterly neat!

The Puzzle of Being

A jigsaw of nonsense, the pieces are rare,
Like socks without partners, or bees without air.
Do we search for the corners or just start to fold?
Each twist and each turn, a new story unfolds.

With laughter in hand, we dive into fate,
Could it be that confusion feels pretty great?
We stumble and fumble, but hey, that's alright,
Let's watch the absurdities dance in the night!

Reason takes naps while chaos runs wild,
Who needs clarity? Let's act like a child!
With giggles as guides, we'll wade through the fray,
As the puzzle gets stranger, we'll laugh all the way.

So here's to the mess, the riddle, the fun,
With lighthearted hearts, we'll outshine the sun.
Amidst all confusion, we'll find what we seek,
In moments so silly, so goofy, so unique!

When Stars Collide

In a cosmic bakery, where stardust is baked,
We whip up confusion, frosting all flaked.
Life's a rich pastry, but oh, what a feat,
With layers so random, we eat and repeat.

Galaxies tumble, like dice in a game,
What's a sun without shadows? Almost too tame!
As stars collide wildly, we giggle and cheer,
In the grand kitchen of chaos, we stir up our fear.

With crumbs of each moment, we share and we squabble,

Trying to figure, yet always a bobble.
What's next in this banquet of whimsical sights?
As we sample existence and dance through the nights!

So toast to the mayhem, the whimsy, the light,
Life's all about laughter, let's keep it in sight.
For when stars collide, it's cosmic delight,
And together we twinkle, so brilliantly bright!

Fragments of a Fleeting Dream

In a café filled with existential dread,
I ordered a latte, but got a loaf instead.
The barista winked, said, "Life's a joke,"
As I pondered the meaning of this almond spoke.

A cat on a roof serenades the moon,
While squirrels debate the best kind of tune.
I laughed at their chatter, what a silly sight,
Yet I wondered, who plays the piano at night?

Do jellybeans know why they're so sweet?
Or do they just roll on in time's endless beat?
With each sugary pop, a new question unfurls,
Life's a candy shop, or just swirling swirls?

In this dream of odd thoughts that swirl with flair,
I lost track of reasons but found a cute bear.
He handed me wisdom in a soft, fuzzy hug,
Saying, "Just enjoy the chaos, you silly mug!"

Echoes of Infinity

A squirrel in a suit talks stocks on a tree,
While pigeons invest in the latest TV.
"Diversify, friends," chirps the bird in a tie,
"Life's just a market, so give it a try."

The stars in the sky blink a code I can't crack,
Like a Wi-Fi password I can't seem to hack.
"Connect to the universe, it's just so divine,"
Said the moon with a smile and a glass of fine wine.

Bubbles in soda cling tight to their dreams,
While lemons debate if they're sweet or just schemes.
In this fizzy realm, everything's fair,
Life's a soft drink, just breathe the fresh air.

I pondered a sandwich, with layers so grand,
Is existential wisdom stuck between bread hand-in-hand?
With each crunchy bite, I just have to reflect,
That sometimes life's answers are found where you least expect.

Tapestry of Dreams

In a world made of yarns, colors swirling about,
Knitting our fates, there's no doubt or pout.
Each stitch a choice, every purl a new day,
Yet the cat steals my yarn, and I'm left in dismay.

The toaster pops up thoughts as I sip my tea,
What if bagels dream of being floats in the sea?
With a whirl and a twirl, I spread on some jam,
Feeling quite whimsical, like I do when I scram.

An octopus sells ice cream just down the block,
With flavors like chaos and a sprinkle of shock.
"Why not?" I pondered, as I giggled a bit,
Isn't life just a scoop? Oh, let's not throw a fit!

In this quilt of odd dreams, so silly and bright,
I found that there's magic in every soft bite.
Let's roll with the nonsense, dance in the breeze,
For life is a party—we'll do as we please!

The Art of Becoming

A blender buzzed loud with secrets to share,
As fruits argued over the best way to flair.
"Life's a smoothie," said kiwi, all fuzzy and wise,
"Blend up your worries, reject your disguise."

Penguins in bowties sip cocoa by the sea,
While debating the purpose of their fancy spree.
"Do we waddle with style, or flippers of grace?
Each splash is a dance, in this quirky embrace!"

Balloon animals float, each one with a dream,
A giraffe wants a necktie, it's all quite supreme.
"Let's inflate our ambitions, rise up to the sky,
Life's a carnival ride—let's give it a try!"

As laughter envelops, I take in the scene,
In this bizarre circus where nothing's routine.
I ponder the magic in every small thing,
Learning that joy's truly the best sort of bling!

Voices in the Stillness

In the silence, whispers play,
Chasing thoughts that run away.
Tiny giggles, echoes loud,
Life's a joke within the crowd.

Ponder paths that lead to bliss,
Finding humor in the miss.
Witty nods from fate's own hand,
Making plans we never planned.

Life's a riddle wrapped in cheer,
With punchlines lurking ever near.
Laughing loud, we dance around,
In silliness, our truth is found.

So let's toast to the absurd,
Raise a glass to the unheard.
For every laugh, a lesson learned,
In the stillness, joy returned.

The Breath Between Thoughts

A pause so brief, we hardly blink,
Where ideas collide and sync.
Chasing thoughts like cats in trees,
Falling over, laughing with ease.

Moments slip just like a sneeze,
Why stress out? Just take it, please!
Every gulp of air a prank,
Life's comedy is never blank.

Dreams linger like the morning fog,
Tripping over metaphors like a dog.
Each thought bubbles like soda pop,
Making us laugh until we flop.

So breathe in deep, forget the rush,
In that pause, we find the hush.
With every breath, a chance to smile,
We dance on life's whimsical aisle.

All the Roads Untaken

So many paths, which one to choose?
Each one ends with funny views.
A stroll through life, a dance in rain,
Misdirection leads to no pain.

The road less traveled might be rough,
But hey, who said it needs to be tough?
With every bump, there's room to play,
In the wrong turn, we find our way.

Mismatched socks and tangled hair,
Life's a puzzle—we're hardly bare.
Each detour sings a quirky tune,
Guiding us like a shining moon.

So let's laugh at what we missed,
In life's grand tale, we persist.
For every fork, a chance to roam,
Adventure calls us all back home.

Every Star a Lost Dream

Watch the stars, they wink and sway,
Telling tales of dreams gone gray.
Each twinkle, a laugh from the past,
In a universe, we're never last.

Glances back at wishes tossed,
It's the journey, not the cost.
With every wish, a hearty chuckle,
Life's a riddle, wrapped in a snuggle.

Stars may fade, but jokes remain,
Like rain on grass, it's all in vain.
These cosmic thoughts do dance and swirl,
Life's an adventure, a crazy whirl.

So raise your eyes to the velvet night,
Every lost dream shines so bright.
In laughter, we find what's right,
Guided by stars in playful flight.

www.ingramcontent.com/pod-product-compliance
Lightning Source LLC
Chambersburg PA
CBHW071845160426
43209CB00003B/427